WALRUSES
OF THE ARCTIC

SARA SWAN MILLER

PowerKiDS
press.
New York

Published in 2009 by The Rosen Publishing Group, Inc.
29 East 21st Street, New York, NY 10010

First Edition

Editor: Amelie von Zumbusch
Book Design: Kate Laczynski
Photo Researcher: Jessica Gerweck

Photo Credits: Cover, back cover (walruses), p. 1 © Sue Flood/Getty Images; back cover (caribou) © www.istockphoto.com/Paul Loewen; back cover (emperor penguins) © www.istockphoto.com/Bernard Breton; back cover (polar bears), p. 4 © www.istockphoto.com/Michel de Nijs; back cover (seals), p. 8 Shutterstock.com; back cover (whales), p. 12 © Paul Nicklen/Getty Images; p. 6 © Thorsten Milse/Getty Images; p. 10 © www.istockphoto.com/John Pitcher; p. 14 © Steven Kazlowski/Peter Arnold, Inc.; p. 16 © www.istockphoto.com/Tersina Shieh; p. 18 © National Geographic/Getty Images; p. 20 © Gaul Dupland/Age Fotostock.com.

Library of Congress Cataloging-in-Publication Data

Miller, Sara Swan.
  Walruses of the arctic / Sara Swan Miller. — 1st ed.
      p. cm. — (Brrr! polar animals)
  Includes index.
  ISBN 978-1-4358-2746-2 (library binding) — ISBN 978-1-4358-3150-6 (pbk.)
ISBN 978-1-4358-3156-8 (6-pack)
  1. Walrus—Arctic regions—Juvenile literature. I. Title.
  QL737.P62M57 2009
  599.79'9—dc22
                                        2008032712

Manufactured in the United States of America

CONTENTS

4

Walruses spend most of their lives in the water. However, they can also be found on beaches, rocky islands, and ice.

WHAT IS A WALRUS?

A walrus is a big **mammal** that lives in the waters of the Arctic. The Arctic is the area around the North Pole. A big male walrus may weigh as much as 2 tons (1,814 kg). It can grow to be 12 feet (4 m) from its nose to the tips of its back **flippers**.

Walruses are in the same family as seals and sea lions. There is just one species, or kind, of walrus. Walruses look a little like seals, but it is easy to tell them apart. Unlike seals, walruses have big square heads, long **tusks**, and **bristles** all around their mouths.

These Atlantic walruses are resting on sea ice off the coast of Spitsbergen, an island in the Arctic Ocean that lies northwest of mainland Norway.

WHERE ARE THE WALRUSES?

There are several populations, or groups, of walruses. These populations live in different places and do not mix. Atlantic walruses live off the coasts of northeastern Canada, Greenland, northern Europe, and northwestern Russia. Pacific walruses live mostly in the waters that border Alaska. Walruses also live in the Laptev Sea, off the coast of northern Russia.

Walruses spend about two-thirds of their time in the water. This is where they find their food. Walruses like fairly **shallow** water with a **gravel** bottom. When walruses haul, or pull, their bodies out of the water, they like to rest on floating sea ice. If there is no ice, walruses will rest on land.

8

The tusks of a male walrus are generally both longer and straighter than those of a female walrus.

LOOKING AT WALRUSES

The first thing most people notice about walruses is their tusks. Both male and female walruses have tusks. A male's tusks can grow to be up to 3 feet (1 m) long. A female's tusks are shorter and not as strong. The tusks grow longer every year. Both males and females use their tusks to help pull themselves up on the ice. Males also use their tusks to fight with other males.

The next thing people generally notice about walruses is the hard bristles around their noses. Walruses use these bristles to feel for their food down on the dark seabed.

This walrus looks pale, or light, because less of the walrus's blood is near its skin. Walruses generally look pale when they are very cold.

IT'S COLD!

It is very cold in the Arctic. The **temperature** there is generally about 5° F (-15° C). Sometimes it gets much colder. Some walruses have been found in water that is -31° F (-35° C)! Luckily, walruses have thick **layers** of fat, called blubber, under their skin. Blubber acts like a coat to keep out the cold and hold in an animal's body heat. In the winter, a walrus's blubber may be 6 inches (15 cm) thick.

When a walrus is in cold water, less of its blood runs near the **surface** of its skin. This also keeps the walrus from losing too much body heat to the water around it.

Walruses find most of their food in waters that are less than 164 feet (50 m) deep.

WHAT'S FOR DINNER?

Walruses eat all kinds of animals that they find on the ocean floor. Walruses dive down in shallow water, using their flippers to swim. They move their back flippers from side to side and **steer** with their front flippers.

Walruses like to eat clams best, but they also like snails, worms, mussels, and other small animals. They feel along the dark seafloor with their bristles. Then, they dig down into the mud with their thick, piglike snouts, or noses. If a clam is buried too deeply, a walrus will shoot water into the clam's **burrow** to uncover it. Then the walrus sucks out the meat.

These walruses have hauled out on a piece of ice in the Chukchi Sea.
The Chukchi Sea lies between Alaska and northeastern Russia.

14

WALRUSES ALL TOGETHER

Walruses love being with other walruses. Hundreds, even thousands, of walruses will haul themselves up on the ice or on land and rest together. They use places called haulouts to do this. Walruses often snuggle, or nuzzle, with each other. They love touching each other with their flippers. Even when it is hot, they huddle together and climb on top of each other. They make deep grunting noises to each other.

Walruses hunt in herds, too. Sometimes they will share food. If one is **attacked**, the other walruses will come to help it. Female walruses will even nurse each other's young.

15

16 *Bulls, or male walruses, use their tusks both to fight over females and to guard their own territory, or space.*

WALRUSES ON THE MOVE

Walrus herds do not stay in the same place all year. When winter is on the way, the walruses head south. They follow the edge of the **ice pack**. Females and males travel in separate herds, but they will meet later in the winter, at **mating** time. When the herds meet in the south, each male gathers a group of females with which to mate. The males use their strong tusks to fight off other males.

When spring begins to return, most of the walruses head north again. They follow the melting edge of the ice pack. The walruses travel hundreds of miles (km) each way.

Baby walruses are called calves. Walrus mothers and calves keep close to each other. The babies sometimes even ride on their mothers' backs.

BABY WALRUSES

Baby walruses are born on the ice from April to June. Mother walruses generally have just one calf at a time. The babies' fur is gray when they are born but turns reddish brown in about two weeks. Newborn walrus babies weigh only around 100 pounds (45 kg), but they grow quickly. Their mothers' milk is rich in fat.

Young walruses stay with their mothers for about two years, nursing all that time. A mother walrus takes wonderful care of her calf. She drives enemies away with her tusks. She will also hold her calf between her front flippers and dive into the water to keep her baby safe.

20 *In the 1800s, nonnative hunters killed many walruses. They made walrus oil with the animals' blubber. The oil was burned in lamps and used to make soap.*

WHO HUNTS WALRUSES?

Even with their mothers guarding them, baby walruses are always in danger. Polar bears hunt them on the land, and killer whales try to catch them in the water. Polar bears and killer whales will also attack grown walruses if they are sick or hurt.

The people who live in the Arctic have hunted walruses for thousands of years. They eat walrus meat and blubber. They use their skins for warm blankets and clothes. Several hundred years ago, other people began hunting walruses. These new hunters killed huge numbers of walruses. The herds almost disappeared, and the native people who counted on the walruses did not have enough to eat.

WILL WALRUSES BE ALL RIGHT?

People finally got worried about what was happening to the walruses. Now, there are laws against hunting these animals. Today, only the people who have always lived in the Arctic are allowed to hunt walruses. The native people hunt just a few animals each year.

Walruses are making a comeback. There are now about 250,000 of them. Still, they face new dangers. The Arctic waters are warming, and the ice is melting. Walruses need the ice pack in their lives. Also, some people are thinking of collecting clams in the Arctic. That would mean less food for walruses. Let's hope that these wonderful animals will live on!

GLOSSARY

attacked (uh-TAKD) Charged at by another animal.

bristles (BRIH-selz) Short, stiff, hairlike fibers.

burrow (BUR-oh) A hole an animal digs in the ground.

flippers (FLIH-perz) Wide, flat body parts that help animals swim.

gravel (GRA-vel) Made of small pieces of rock.

ice pack (EYES PAK) Pieces of floating ice that cover much of the water at Earth's poles.

layers (LAY-erz) Thicknesses of something.

mammal (MA-mul) A warm-blooded animal that has a backbone and hair, breathes air, and feeds milk to its young.

mating (MAY-ting) Coming together to make babies.

shallow (SHA-loh) Not deep.

steer (STEER) To guide something's path.

surface (SER-fes) The outside of anything.

temperature (TEM-pur-cher) How hot or cold something is.

tusks (TUSKS) Long, large pointed teeth that come out of the mouths of some animals.

INDEX

WEB SITES

Due to the changing nature of Internet links, PowerKids Press has developed an online list of Web sites related to the subject of this book. This site is updated regularly. Please use this link to access the list:
www.powerkidslinks.com/brrr/walrus/